REBELS WITH A CAUSE

CAMPAIGNERS

By Paul Thomas

 Belitha Press

First published in Great Britain in 1997 by

Belitha Press Limited,
London House, Great Eastern Wharf,
Parkgate Road, London SW11 4NQ

Editor: Veronica Ross
Series designer: Hayley Cove
Designer: Steve Wilson
Picture researcher: Diana Morris
Consultant: Hazel Mary Martell
Cover Illustrator: Mac McIntosh

ISBN 1 85561 552 5

Printed in Portugal

British Library Cataloguing in Publication Data
CIP data for this book is available from the British Library.

Photographic credits
AKG, London: 8t Musée Carnavalet; 23b, 27t. Archive Photos: 21b, 29t;/Express Newspapers 36b, 40b; 44b. Associated Press/Jackson Daily News/Fred Blackwell: 44b. Bridgeman Art Library: /Giraudon 9 Chateau de Versailles; 10 William Penn House. Brown Brothers : 32b, 33. Camera Press: 26, 31b, 39b. Colorific!/Black Star:/Fred Ward 42; /Charles Moore 43b.Corbis-Bettmann: /UPI 4; 16t, 19b, 20, 25t, 30, 31t, 34; /Reuters 41; /UPI 43t. Environmental Picture Library: 5b. Mary Evans Picture Library: 6, 11b, 22t, 22b, 24.Robert Harding Picture Agency:/Gavin Heller 35b. Hulton Getty Collection: 12, 13t, 23t, 25b, 29b. Mansell Collection: 8b. Moviestore Collection: 27b.Peter Newark's Pictures: 11t, 13b, 15, 16b, 17, 19t, 21t. North Wind Pictures: 7t, 7b, 14, 18. Novosti (London): 35t. Popperfoto: 5t, 28, 38, 39t. Redferns:/Ebet Roberts 32t. Rex Features: 40t. Frank Spooner/Gamma:/Kaku Kurita 36b;/Ferry-Liaison 37. Topham Picture Source:/AP 44t.

Words in **bold** appear in the glossary on page 46.

Contents

INTRODUCTION

All over the world, people campaign to change unjust laws, or to support a cause that they feel strongly about. In this book, we tell ten fascinating life stories of people who fought for change, and made an impact on world history.

Political campaigners

Thomas Paine was one of the greatest political thinkers of the eighteenth century. He campaigned for freedom and equality, and spoke out against slavery. A later political campaigner was Marcus Garvey. In the 1920s, he told black people to be proud of their African history.

The nineteenth century

One of the most successful campaigns was the fight to end slavery in America. Frederick Douglass and John Brown were leaders of the anti-slavery movement which led to the **abolition** of slavery in 1865. In Britain at this time Elizabeth Fry was campaigning for better prison conditions.

Peaceful protest

Twentieth-century campaigners used **civil disobedience** to draw attention to their cause. The Pankhursts chained themselves to buildings to publicize their campaign to win the vote for women. In India, Gandhi refused to obey British rule; while in America, black American supporters of Martin Luther King sat in 'whites only' bus seats and refused to move.

Martin Luther King leads a protest against **segregation** in the USA.

Ban the bomb

Not all campaigns achieve their aims. The Campaign for Nuclear Disarmament (CND) has not been successful in its campaign to rid the world of nuclear weapons. But campaigns will continue to happen whenever people feel that a wrong in society can be changed by protest.

A CND march in London in 1983. The campaigners were protesting against American **cruise missiles** in England.

Campaigning on

Some campaigns carry on for many years. Environmental campaigner Jacques Cousteau has been fighting for more than 30 years to protect our planet, its wildlife and natural resources from pollution.

In South Africa, Nelson Mandela campaigned for over 50 years for the abolition of apartheid. In 1962, he was sentenced to life in prison. Mandela was released when a world-wide protest against apartheid forced the South African government to change its attitude.

Environmental group Greenpeace try to stop a Norwegian ship from catching and killing whales.

THOMAS PAINE

1737–1809

Thomas Paine, writer and political thinker, campaigned for equality, freedom and an end to poverty. He was one of the most influential people in eighteenth-century Europe and America.

Thomas Paine was born in 1737 in Norfolk. His early life was marked by failures. He trained as a corset maker, and opened his own shop. But the business did badly, and he was forced to close it down. His next job was as an **excise** officer, tracking down smugglers, and collecting taxes on alcohol and tobacco. The wages were poor, and Paine was sacked for asking for a pay rise. His private life was also unhappy. His first wife died, and his second marriage ended in separation.

Adventure seeker

Paine decided to try his luck in London. While he was there, he met the American politician Benjamin Franklin, who advised him to go America. Paine had a burning desire for adventure, so he took Franklin's advice. He arrived in America in 1774, and found a job on the *Pennsylvania Magazine*. He became interested in journalism, and wrote articles against slavery, and in support of women's rights.

Political author and thinker Thomas Paine wanted a world in which everyone would be free and equal.

American Independence

The history of the United States of America began on 4 July 1776, when 13 English **colonies** on the eastern coast of North America declared themselves independent from British rule. The **Congress** of American Colonies drew up the Declaration of Independence which said that the colonies were free from British control. This painting shows colonists drafting the declaration.

Best seller

In 1775, the American Revolution had reached its height. Paine played an active role. In his book *Common Sense*, which was published in 1775, Paine said that Americans should cut all links with Britain, and demand complete independence. The book became a best seller, and more than 500 000 copies were sold in just a few months. Many Americans were not sure that breaking away from Britain was the right thing to do, but *Common Sense* helped to persuade them that it was.

The Crisis papers

Between 1776 and 1783, Paine wrote the 16 Crisis papers. During the long, cold winter of 1776-77, these pamphlets were handed out to the American troops to encourage them to continue the fight for freedom. The first pamphlet, called *The American Crisis*, opened with the words 'These are the times that try men's souls.'

Rebel American forces fighting English soldiers at the Battle of the Brandywine during the American Revolution.

The French Revolution

In 1789, riots broke out in Paris. French citizens were tired of paying high taxes to support the lavish lifestyle of King Louis XVI and his wife Marie Antoinette. In July 1789 angry crowds stormed the Bastille, an ancient prison and symbol of royal power. They demanded an end to the monarchy, and the establishment of a French **republic**. The king and queen, and thousands of nobles were executed in a violent reaction to the old system of rule.

Poverty stricken

Despite the success of his book, Paine was penniless after the war. He made no money on his books and papers because he wanted them to be sold as cheaply as possible so that everyone would be able to buy them. George Washington, leader of the American army and first president of the United States of America, realized the important role that Thomas Paine had played in the American Revolution. He helped him to find somewhere to live, and gave him a pension.

The Rights of Man

But Tom Paine was not a man to settle into early retirement. In 1789, he returned to England where he wrote *The Rights of Man,* in support of the French Revolution. Paine believed that monarchies should be abolished in favour of republics. In the same book, he called for an end to poverty, **illiteracy** and unemployment. He also described his ideas for pensions for elderly people, education for children, and poor relief.

Found guilty

These ideas were thought to be **radical** and dangerous. The book was banned in England, and the publisher sent to prison. Orders went out for Paine's arrest, but he escaped to France. He was tried in his absence, found guilty and declared an outlaw.

An eighteenth-century political cartoon passing judgement on Tom Paine. Many people thought he was mad and dangerous.

In August 1792, French revolutionaries stormed the Tuileries, where Louis XVI was living, and imprisoned the royal family.

Imprisoned in France

Paine stayed in France, and was elected a member of the National Convention, which was the new revolutionary parliament. He joined in the call for the **abolition** of the French monarchy, but he spoke out against the violence and the large number of executions. In 1793, Paine was thrown into prison because he tried to stop the revolutionaries executing Louis XVI.

During this time, Thomas Paine wrote his last great work, *The Age of Reason.* In this book he attacked religion, which he said was just superstition. Paine was released from prison after about a year. He stayed in France after his release and rejoined the National Convention.

Changing times

In 1802, Paine returned to America, but times had changed and the American people had forgotten his contribution to the American Revolution. They were angry about his attacks on Christianity in *The Age of Reason*, and for the last few years of his life Tom Paine was forgotten and ignored. He died on 8 June 1809.

Radical ideas

Thomas Paine spent his life campaigning for freedom and basic human rights. Many of his ideas, such as his plans for popular education, relief of the poor, and pensions, were ahead of their time, and considered too radical to be taken seriously. But his influence was far-reaching. During the twentieth century, Paine has been rightly recognized as one of the greatest political campaigners in history.

ELIZABETH FRY

1780–1845

English prison reformer Elizabeth Fry spent her life campaigning to improve conditions in prisons throughout Britain and Europe.

In the seventeenth and eighteenth centuries, conditions in English prisons were appalling. The cells were filthy and overcrowded, with men and women packed in together. Many prisoners died of diseases, such as cholera and typhus, that they caught in prison.

People were imprisoned for committing even minor crimes, such as stealing a loaf of bread. Other prisoners were people who were mentally ill. They should not have been in prison at all, but there was nowhere else for them to go.

School teacher

Elizabeth Gurney was born in Norwich in 1780. She was the daughter of a wealthy Quaker banker, and she grew up in a large, happy family. When she was 17, Elizabeth began visiting the poor people in her village. She soon became aware of the differences between her life and the lives of the villagers. She tried to think of ways to help, and set up a school so that she could teach the local children to read and write. In 1800, she married Joseph Fry, a Quaker and local merchant.

Elizabeth Fry, one of the most important campaigners for prison reform in Europe.

Shocking conditions

In 1813, Stephen Grellet, an American friend of Elizabeth's and a fellow Quaker, visited Newgate Prison in London. He was shocked by what he saw. Men, women and children shared the same cells, and all the prisoners had lice and fleas. The children were thin and underfed, and ran around half-naked. One cell housed 300 women. Many of them were drunk, and they were fighting and swearing.

Improving the prisons

Grellet described what he had seen to Elizabeth. She could not believe what he told her, and decided to visit Newgate to see for herself. The prison was exactly as Grellet had described it. Elizabeth was so horrified that she decided she must try to help the prisoners and improve conditions in the prison.

Elizabeth Fry visiting female prisoners in Newgate Prison. Many of the women were so violent that the prison governor refused to walk among them.

Quakers

The real name for the Quakers is The Society of Friends. The society was formed in the seventeenth century, and later spread to Africa, Asia and America. Friends do not have clergymen because they believe that everyone has a special relationship with God. They hold meetings, but they do not say prayers or sing hymns. Friends are pacifists and believe that education is very important. They also believe in equality for everyone.

Better conditions

Fry complained to the prison authorities and told them that they should make sure that the food was nutritious, especially for the children in prison.

She collected bundles of old clothes from her friends and family, and gave the women sewing materials and cloth so that they could mend their old clothes, and make new ones for themselves and their children. The women were also allowed to make patchwork quilts which they could sell to make a little money.

Fry set up a school in Newgate Prison, and taught the prisoners how to read and write. At first the prison authorities opposed her work, thinking that the prisoners would not appreciate it. But Fry was able to show them that the prisoners behaved better when they were treated well.

New laws

As a result of Fry's campaign, the British parliament introduced laws to improve the conditions in all prisons. Women warders were employed to look after women prisoners, men and women had separate cells, and all jails were inspected regularly.

Convict ships

British prisons were so overcrowded that many prisoners were sent to **penal colonies** in Australia. The journey by ship took several weeks, and the conditions on board were terrible because so many prisoners were packed into a small area. Fry visited 106 convict ships before they left for Australia, and forced the authorities to allow enough space for the prisoners to move around. She succeeded in transforming the convicts' voyage.

Teaching prisoners to read the *Bible* in Newgate Prison in 1814.

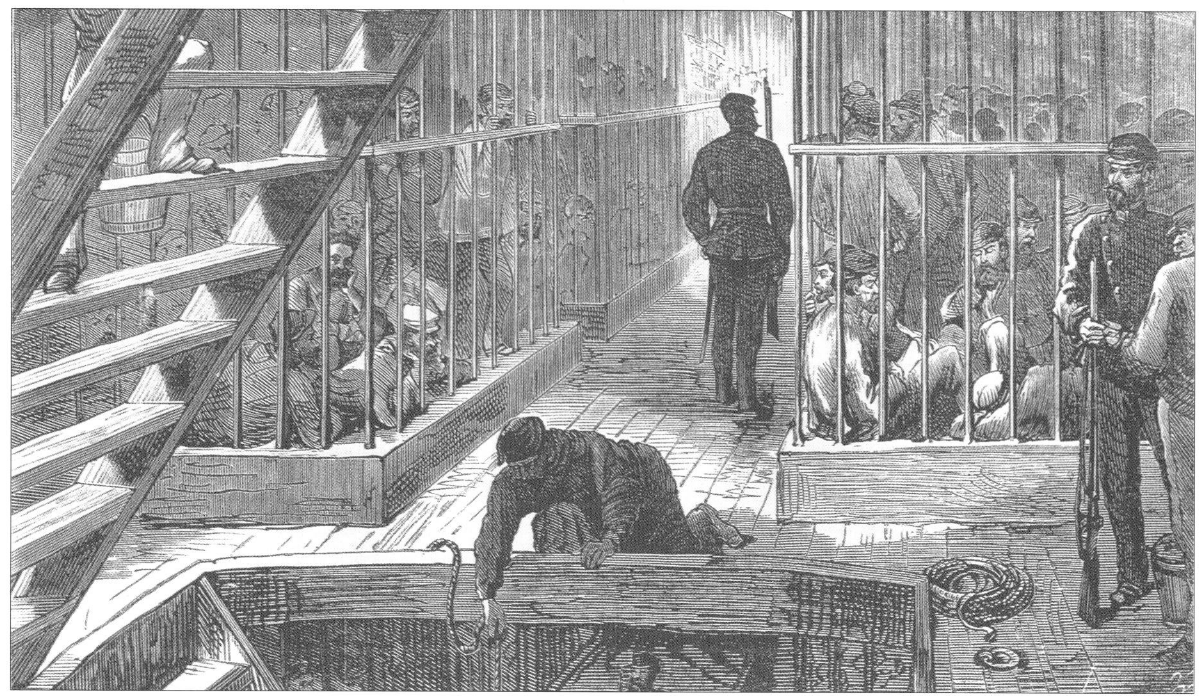

Prisoners caged like animals on board a convict ship bound for Botany Bay, Australia.

International fame

Fry's fame as a campaigner and prison reformer spread to other countries. Between 1818 and 1843 she visited prisons in Ireland, France, Belgium, the Netherlands, Prussia and Denmark. Wherever she went people asked her how they could improve their prisons.

Mourned by thousands

Ill-health finally forced Fry to stop travelling. She remained an invalid for the last few years of her life, and died in 1845. Thousands of people gathered at her funeral to mourn her death.

Prisons

Today, the most common form of punishment for people who commit serious crimes is imprisonment. But a prison sentence for a criminal offence is quite a modern development. Until the eighteenth century, most criminals were likely to be whipped, branded with a hot iron, or even executed. Prisons were used mainly for political prisoners who were held because of their beliefs.

JOHN BROWN

1800–1859

John Brown is an unusual figure in American history. He was a white man who fought for the freedom of black slaves in the United States of America.

John Brown was born in Connecticut, USA, in 1800, but his family moved to Ohio when he was five years old. John's father owned a leather **tannery**, and when John left school he went to work for his father and then set up in business on his own.

Financial hardship

John Brown was a poor businessman, and he struggled to make enough money to support his wife and children. He invested money in land only to lose most of it when prices dropped. Then he started a sheep farm, but that went bankrupt in 1842. Most of the time his family suffered terrible financial hardships.

The search for a better life

Brown and his family moved several times in search of a better life. In 1849, they settled in a black community at North Elba, New York, on land donated by an anti-slavery supporter. Despite his own hardships, Brown could see that many black people were far worse off.

Militant anti-slavery campaigner John Brown helped to bring about the abolition of slavery in the United States of America.

Slave state

At this time, many Africans living in the USA were still slaves. Some of the northern states had **abolished** slavery, and former slaves had found work on building sites, or in factories. But their wages were so low that they could not afford to feed their families, and the conditions they lived in were little better than slavery.

In 1855, Brown moved to Kansas, where slavery was still legal. He became involved in the anti-slavery movement, and joined in peaceful protests calling for freedom for all black men and women.

Violent times

But when an anti-slavery supporter was murdered and the culprit allowed to go free, Brown decided that peaceful protests were a waste of time. He soon became convinced that the only way to fight the injustice of slavery was with violence.

Pottawatomie Creek

One night in May 1856, John Brown, and four of his sons, rode into Pottawatomie Creek in Kansas to raid a pro-slavery settlement. Five people were murdered. The massacre had the effect Brown hoped it would. More and more people joined the anti-slavery movement, and fighting broke out between anti-slavery and pro-slavery forces. Finally, the American government agreed to abolish slavery in Kansas.

Slave labour

About six million Africans were transported to America during the eighteenth century. They were sold at auctions, and taken to work on the plantations where they were used as slave labour to cultivate crops of tobacco, cotton and sugar cane. During the nineteenth century, many people began to campaign against slavery. Former slaves were encouraged to tell their stories, and to describe the beatings and cruel treatment they had experienced at the hands of their owners. This early photograph, taken in about 1860, shows a family of slaves working in the fields.

John Brown preparing to fight as United States marines break down the door of the armoury at Harper's Ferry.

Harper's Ferry

Brown turned his attention to the abolition of slavery in other southern states. In 1859, with a band of armed supporters, Brown captured a government **armoury** at Harper's Ferry in West Virginia. Harper's Ferry was the entrance to the Great Black Way. This was the route slaves used to escape from the slavery of the southern states to freedom in the north.

Brown hoped that news of his attack would spread, and that slaves in the area would join him. His plan was to give them guns from the armoury and start a slave revolt. About three of the four million slaves in the United States lived in this area, and Brown thought that such a large number would make a revolt unstoppable.

Uprising and capture

But the uprising did not go according to plan. Government troops surrounded the armoury and stopped the rebels passing the weapons out to their supporters.

After two days, United States marines stormed the building. The government wanted to capture the rebels, dead or alive. Ten men were killed, including two of Brown's sons, and John Brown and the rest of the group were captured.

Day of execution

The rebels were tried for murder, slave **insurrection** and **treason** against the state. They were sentenced to death. On 2 December 1859, Brown kissed his wife and family goodbye, and visited his companions for the last time. Then he was led out to be hanged.

More than 3000 soldiers formed a 25 kilometre circle around the scaffold to keep back Brown's supporters, and to stop any last minute attempts to rescue him.

The Last Moments of John Brown by Thomas Hovenden (1884). Brown became a hero after his death. The song *John Brown's Body* was a marching song for Union troops in the American Civil War.

Nat Turner

One of the most famous revolts against slavery was led by Nat Turner, a black slave. Turner believed that through violence he would win freedom for all slaves. In August 1831, Turner and six other slaves killed their owner. Over the next two months, 56 white people were murdered. Turner was captured in October 1831, and executed. John Brown was influenced by this revolt, which changed the idea that slaves were content in their chains.

The abolition of slavery

John Brown met his death calmly and bravely. For many Americans he was a **martyr** who had sacrificed his life in the fight for freedom. His actions helped to spread the call for the abolition of slavery throughout the United States. Slavery was finally abolished in 1865.

Frederick Douglass

1817–1895

Frederick Douglass, former slave and anti-slavery campaigner, became one of the most important human rights leaders of the nineteenth century.

Frederick Bailey was born into slavery in Maryland, USA in 1817. He was separated from his mother when he was a baby, and sent to live with his grandmother. When he was aged seven or eight, he was sold to Hugh Auld, a slave-owner from Baltimore.

This move was an important turning-point in Frederick's life. He was sent to work as a servant in the plantation house where he made friends with Auld's wife, Sophie. She ignored the state law, which said that slaves must not be educated, and taught Frederick to read. Many years later, Frederick said that learning to read was his 'pathway from slavery to freedom'.

Unfit for slavery

Hugh Auld was angry when he found out that Frederick could read. He told his wife that black people should not be educated because it made them unfit for slavery and gave them ideas about escaping. As a punishment, Auld sent Frederick to work for Edward Covey, a violent man who enjoyed beating slaves.

Frederick Douglass was the first black American to hold high office in the United States government.

Slave hunters and their dogs chasing an escaped slave.

Learning to write

But Frederick stood up to Covey's brutal treatment. One day he told Covey that if he hit him once more he would fight him until one of them was killed. Covey realized he would never break Frederick's spirit, and he sent him back to Hugh Auld's plantation in Baltimore.

Auld died shortly after Frederick's return, and Frederick was sent away to learn ship **caulking**. He taught himself to write by tracing the letters on the **prows** of the ships.

Escape from slavery

Frederick made his first attempt to escape from slavery when he was 16, but his plans were discovered before he could get away. Five years later, disguised as a free black seaman, Frederick caught a train to New York City. He changed his surname to Douglass to hide his real identity. He had escaped, but he was not a free man.

NARRATIVE

OF THE

LIFE

OF

FREDERICK DOUGLASS,

AN

AMERICAN SLAVE.

WRITTEN BY HIMSELF.

BOSTON:

PUBLISHED AT THE ANTI-SLAVERY OFFICE.

No. 25 CORNHILL

1845.

Slave autobiographies

Between 1820 and 1860, many books were written by slaves about their lives. They described the slaves' experiences on the plantations, their escape to freedom, and their attempts to **abolish** slavery. The most popular books were written by Frederick Douglass, Moses Roper and Solomon Northup. They sold thousands of copies, and were translated into many languages.

Publishing a best seller

Douglass moved to Massachusetts, where he became involved in the campaign to abolish slavery. In 1841, he told his life story at an anti-slavery meeting. Douglass spoke so well that many people could not believe that he had been a slave. His lectures became very popular, and he was encouraged to write the story of his life. This was published in 1845 as *The Narrative of the Life of Frederick Douglass, An American Slave.* The book became a best seller.

Lecture tour

Douglass left the USA to escape the slave hunters, and went on a lecture tour of Great Britain and Ireland. During the tour, he made many friends, and they raised the money for him to buy his freedom.

Abraham Lincoln

During his campaign to be elected president of the United States in 1860, Abraham Lincoln spoke out against slavery. He believed that slavery was evil and should be abolished. But the economy in the southern states relied heavily on the slaves who worked on the plantations where crops of sugar cane and cotton were grown. Many southerners were against Lincoln's policy to abolish slavery, and in 1865, he was shot and killed by a fanatical supporter of the southern states.

The North Star

When he returned to the USA, Douglass started an anti-slavery newspaper, called the *North Star,* to put forward his views. He was a brilliant journalist and wrote many articles about the evils of slavery. Douglass also campaigned for the **civil rights** of free black people. They had been released from slavery, but many found it difficult to find work because they were **discriminated** against.

A nineteenth-century etching showing Frederick Douglass, writer and statesman, at work in his office in Washington DC.

Lincoln's wartime consultant

During the war, President Lincoln asked Douglass to work with him as a consultant. Douglass said that former slaves should be armed and allowed to fight. He helped to raise two **regiments** of black soldiers, and his three sons joined the army.

Ambassador to Haiti

Slavery was finally abolished in 1865. After the war, Douglass held several positions in the American government. In 1889, he became the American ambassador to Haiti. He was the first black person to have such an important job.

Douglass' powerful speeches and his work in government helped to end slavery and improve the lives of black people in the USA. In 1895, at the age of 78, Douglass died of a heart attack in Washington DC.

War breaks out

In 1861 the American Civil War broke out. The war split the United States in two as north and south fought over the issue of slavery. In the northern states of America, all black people were free, but in the southern states, black people were still slaves. The war began when some of the southern states broke away from the United States and formed the Confederacy. At first the Confederates seemed to be winning, but the northern army fought back and defeated the Confederacy in 1865.

A photograph of the 107th US infantry taken during the American Civil War. It was America's first black regiment.

THE PANKHURSTS

EMMELINE PANKHURST 1858–1928

CHRISTABEL PANKHURST 1880–1958

Emmeline and Christabel Pankhurst were the leaders of the **suffragette** movement that campaigned to win the vote for women in Britain.

Towards the end of the nineteenth century there was a growing interest in women's rights, and women all over the world began to campaign for the right to vote. Women in New Zealand won the vote in 1893, and Australia followed in 1902. But in Britain, most men thought that politics should not concern women.

At this time, British women had very few rights. It was difficult for them to take up a profession, go to university, or become involved in politics.

The Pankhurst family

In Britain the Pankhurst family, led by Emmeline Pankhurst and her daughters Christabel, Sylvia and Adele, began the fight for the vote.

Emmeline was born in Manchester in 1858. She studied in Paris, and returned to England to marry Richard Pankhurst, a lawyer. In 1889, Emmeline helped to set up the Women's Franchise League. In 1894, this won the right for married women to vote in local elections.

Militant campaigners for women's suffrage Emmeline Pankhurst (top) and her daughter Christabel.

Votes for women!

In 1903, Emmeline set up the Women's Social and Political Union (WSPU) to campaign for women's suffrage. Before long the women were called suffragettes. The union's slogan was 'Deeds not Words', and from the very beginning the Pankhursts organized marches and demonstrations. They burst into political meetings waving banners and shouting 'votes for women'.

A militant campaign

But these protests did not achieve very much. Christabel convinced her mother that the suffragettes should become more militant. So the women launched a new campaign and went to great lengths to have their cause taken seriously.

Emmeline Pankhurst being carried away by police after a suffragette attack on Buckingham Palace in May 1914.

Resisting arrest

They chained themselves to lamp posts and smashed shop windows, and when the police were called to the scene, the women resisted arrest. In 1913, Emily Davison threw herself under the King's horse at the Derby, and was killed. These incidents brought the suffragettes publicity, and made people aware of their campaign.

The women's movement

During the twentieth century, women's organizations continued to campaign for equal pay, education and job opportunities. Laws have been passed in Europe and America, which ban sex **discrimination** in places of work. But there are still very few women in top jobs, and throughout the world women continue to earn less than their male colleagues for doing the same work.

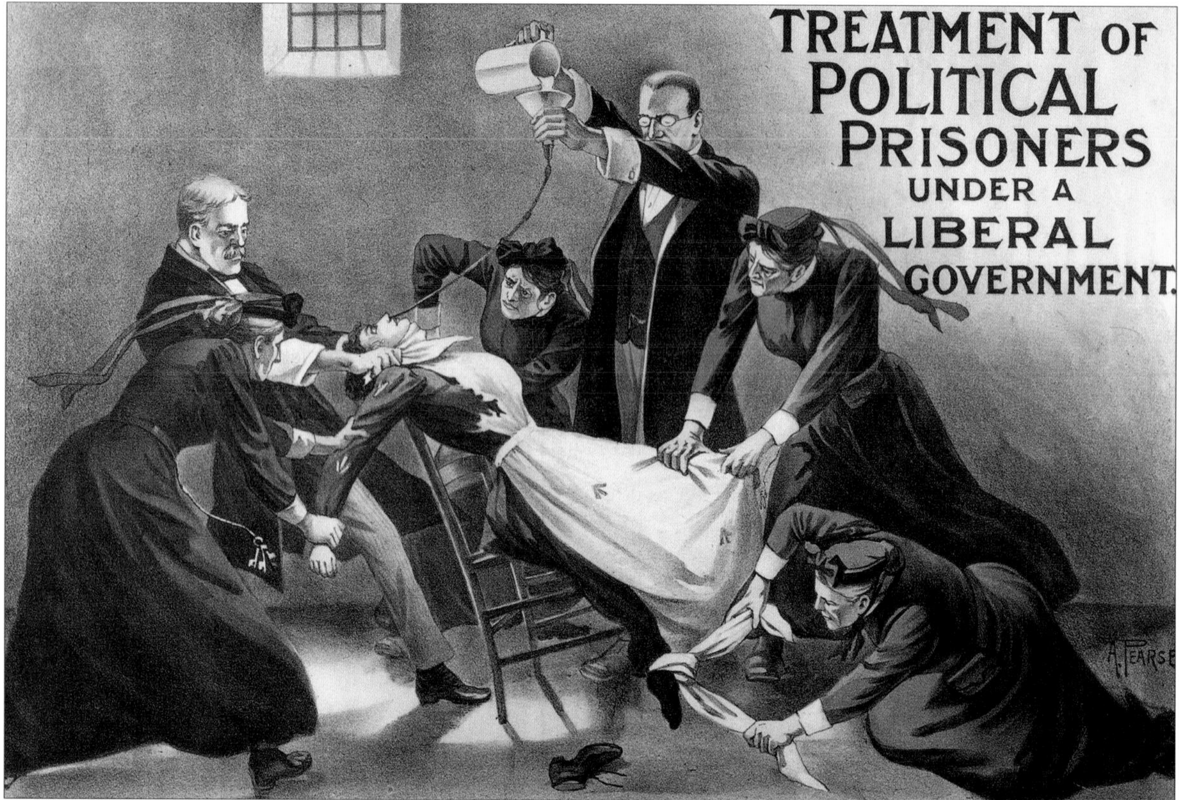

A dramatic suffragette poster from the early 1900s criticising the government's policy of force-feeding women in prison.

Government action

The women in prison carried on their protest by going on hunger strike. But the British government took firm action against them, and the women were force-fed. People were outraged when they saw how the suffragettes were treated.

Cat and Mouse

In 1913, the Prisoners (Temporary Discharge for Ill-Health) Act was passed. It was nicknamed the Cat and Mouse Act. Under this act, women hunger strikers were released from prison when they became ill, but re-arrested as soon as they were better. This happened to Emmeline Pankhurst 12 times. On one occasion she went to a suffragette meeting on a stretcher.

War breaks out

Such determination brought the suffragette movement so much support that it seemed women would soon get the vote. But in 1914 the First World War broke out. The government released all the suffragettes who were still in prison, and the Pankhursts called off the campaign. Emmeline and Christabel knew that the suffragettes would lose a lot of support if they carried on challenging the government while the country was at war. Instead, they advised women to support the war effort and go to work for their country.

The First World War 1914-1918

In June 1914 Archduke Ferdinand, heir to the Austrian throne, was murdered by a Serbian **nationalist**. This event triggered the start of the First World War. Within weeks, Austria had declared war on Serbia, and Europe was split into two camps. Russia went to the aid of the Serbs, along with its allies Britain and France, and Germany declared war on Russia. Other European powers soon allied with one side or the other. Millions of men went to fight, and more than ten million people were killed.

Women at war

The suffragettes took jobs in factories making weapons and ammunition, and helped run public services, such as the postal service. The war was the first time that many women had worked, and they proved that they could do the job, as well as, if not better than, men. When the war ended in 1918, public support was behind the suffragette movement, and women over the age of 30 were given the vote. In 1928, the age was lowered to 21, which finally put women on an equal footing with men.

Freedom fighters

The Pankhursts made a huge contribution to the freedom of women by fighting for the right to vote. After the war, Emmeline lectured on child welfare. Christabel settled in America, and wrote her life story, *Unshackled: The story of how we won the vote.*

A woman working in a **munitions** factory during the First World War.

MAHATMA GANDHI

1869–1948

Political and religious leader Mahatma Gandhi inspired millions of Indians to join him in his campaign to win independence for India.

In the 1850s about two-thirds of India was ruled by Britain. The Raj (the British government in India) made all the decisions about how India should be run. But towards the end of the nineteenth century, a new **nationalist** movement began to take hold in India. Members of the movement believed that Indians should be in charge of their own country, and that it was time for the British to go. In 1885 the Indian National **Congress** campaigned for small changes in government. When these changes were refused, they started to campaign for home rule.

Young lawyer

Mohandas Karamchand Gandhi was born in 1869 in Porbandar, western India. His father and grandfather were local officials in the Raj. Gandhi was married when he was just 14. In 1887, he left his wife and son in India, and went to London to study law. He returned to India in 1891, and tried to make a living as a lawyer. But the legal profession was very overcrowded, and it was difficult for him to find a job.

Gandhi was determined to free India from British rule. His non-violent protests persuaded Indians to join his fight for freedom.

Racial discrimination

After two years, Gandhi accepted a job with an Indian law firm in South Africa. Many Asian people lived in South Africa. They had **emigrated** to find jobs, but they were disliked by the white South Africans. Soon after Gandhi's arrival in South Africa, he suffered **racial harassment** because he was not white. He was thrown off a train, and refused entry to hotels.

Gandhi protested at the way Asians were treated, and began a campaign against racial **discrimination**. He led peaceful protests and refused to use violence. He said 'I am prepared to die, but I am not prepared to kill.' He was arrested and thrown into prison, but he never hit back at his enemies.

Gandhi outside his law office in South Africa.

A simple life

When Gandhi returned to India in 1915, the Indian National Congress had become more **militant**. They wanted the British to leave India. They asked Gandhi to become their leader, but he refused. He wanted to live a simple life on his farm, where he grew his own food, and spun yarn to make clothes.

Political leader

Gandhi did not want to become involved in politics, but he changed his mind in 1919. This was the year of the Amritsar Massacre, when hundreds of Indians were killed by the British Army.

The Amritsar Massacre

In April 1919 a crowd of unarmed Indians in Amritsar, northern India, protested against British rule. General Dyer, a British officer, thought the protesters were threatening and ordered his soldiers to open fire. Nearly 400 people were killed. The massacre made the cause of Indian independence more popular in India and throughout the world. This picture is from the film *Gandhi,* released in 1982.

Boycotting the British

Gandhi decided that he must take direct action. He agreed to become the leader of the Indian National Congress, and in 1920 he launched a policy of **non-co-operation** with the British. He encouraged Indians to **boycott** British goods. Many Indians gave up their jobs in local government and refused to obey British authorities. They sat and blocked the streets, refusing to move even when they were beaten by police.

Hunger strike

Gandhi was arrested several times, and each time he went on a hunger strike as part of his campaign of **civil disobedience**. The British authorities found it hard to deal with him because he was never angry or violent.

The Salt March

The Salt March was the most spectacular campaign against British rule in India. In 1930 Gandhi led thousands of people on a 385 kilometre walk to the coast, where he took salt from sea water. This was in direct protest against the British government tax on salt. Everyone in India was made to buy salt from the state even though they could make it very cheaply themselves.

Religious problems

In 1922, Gandhi was imprisoned for two years. When he was released, he decided to withdraw from politics. The continual fighting between India's two main religious groups, the Muslims and the Hindus, was a major problem for Gandhi. They found it impossible to live peacefully together, and this made it very difficult to unite India in the struggle for independence.

The ruined remains of a house owned by a rich Hindu banker that was destroyed by Muslims.

Violent explosion

The religious conflict was still a problem. Gandhi tried to find a solution, but the differences between the Hindus and Muslims were too great. In 1947, India was **partitioned**, and Pakistan was created as a separate Muslim state. Millions of people were forced to leave their homes, and there was an explosion of violence between the Hindus and Muslims. Millions were killed.

Gandhi's funeral procession passes through Bombay. His ashes were scattered in 50 rivers in India and Pakistan.

Independence for India

Gandhi re-entered politics in 1930, and launched a second campaign of non-co-operation. Finally, the British agreed to begin talks on India's self-government, and in 1947 India became independent.

Great soul

Gandhi was against partition, and his disappointment that India had been divided made the Hindus very angry. In January 1948, Gandhi was **assassinated** at a peace rally in Delhi by a Hindu **extremist**. Although he died violently, Gandhi's message was that peaceful protests always win in the end. He is known all over the world as Mahatma, which means great soul.

MARCUS GARVEY

1887–1940

Jamaican campaigner Marcus Garvey organized one of the first black **nationalist** movements to fight for the rights of black people. He is remembered as a national hero in Jamaica.

During the seventeenth and eighteenth centuries, millions of Africans were captured and transported to America where they were sold into slavery. When slavery was **abolished** in 1865, many Africans dreamed of returning to their homelands where they could live in freedom. But by 1900, most of Africa was governed by European powers, such as Britain, France and Germany. Only Liberia and Ethiopia remained independent.

Strike leader

Marcus Garvey was born on the Caribbean island of Jamaica in 1887. When he was 14, he left school to become a printer's apprentice. A few years later, he took a job with a printing firm in the capital, Kingston, where he led a strike for higher wages and better working conditions. After the strike Garvey lost his job. Finding another one was difficult as employers regarded him as a troublemaker. So Garvey decided to leave Jamaica for Central America.

Marcus Garvey at the height of his power in 1920. His followers called him Black Moses.

Booker T Washington

Booker T Washington was born into slavery in America in 1856. When he was a young man slavery was abolished, and he was able to go to college where he trained to become a teacher. Washington believed that education was more important than anything else. With the help of his students, he built his own college for black students at Tuskegee, Alabama. Washington's autobiography *Up from Slavery* has been a great influence on many black leaders in the twentieth century.

African culture

In 1912, Garvey travelled to London where he read *Up from Slavery*, the autobiography of Booker T Washington. The book captured Garvey's imagination. He became interested in African history, and in the struggle of African people to escape from slavery.

Back to Africa

Garvey believed that Africans should be proud of their traditions. In London, he met people who talked about African customs and beliefs, and traditions of art and music. He began to dream about creating a black-governed nation in Africa.

In 1914, Garvey returned to Jamaica, where he set up the Universal Negro Improvement Association (UNIA). The organization wanted to improve the living standards of black people everywhere, and encourage black people to return to their native lands where they would build a black nation. This movement was called Back to Africa.

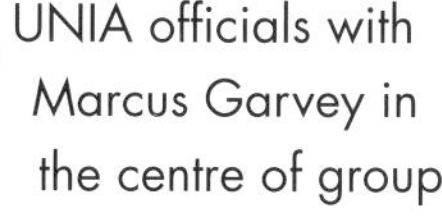

UNIA officials with Marcus Garvey in the centre of group.

A growing organization

Garvey travelled to the USA to win support for his organization. He was a powerful speaker, and in a short time he gained a large following. He told black people that they could do great things if they believed in themselves and worked together. Branches of the UNIA were set up all over America and Africa.

Garvey raised money by opening grocery stores, restaurants, a newspaper, and The Black Star Line, a fleet of steamships that would return people to Africa.

Street parade

At the peak of his power, Marcus Garvey had about one million followers. In 1920, he headed an international conference in New York with representatives from 25 countries. The conference ended with a parade through the streets of Harlem.

Shattered dreams

But some of Garvey's business methods came under suspicion and, in 1923, he was arrested for **fraud**. He was found guilty and imprisoned for two years. In 1927, he was **deported** to Jamaica.

Garvey was a deeply disappointed man. The UNIA had been banned in African countries, and his plans for a black-run nation in Africa lay in ruins. In 1935 he returned to London, where he tried to start a new movement, but it failed. Marcus Garvey died in poverty in 1940.

Marcus Garvey, handcuffed to a police officer, is led away after his arrest for fraud.

Rastafarians

Marcus Garvey was a major force behind the Rastafarian movement, which began in Jamaica in the 1930s. Rastafarians believed that Haile Selassie, or Ras Tafari, Emperor of Ethiopia was the living God. The movement is named after him. For many Africans, Ethiopia is the birthplace of African nationalism. Rastafarians have their own musical style called reggae. Bob Marley, left, was a Rastafarian. He became one of the most famous musicians in the world.

Hope for the future

Since his death, Marcus Garvey has become one of the best known black leaders of the twentieth century. He brought pride, self-respect and hope for the future to black people all over the world by teaching them about their African heritage. In 1962, when Jamaica became independent, Marcus Garvey was named as one of the island's national heroes. His tomb, which stands in a park in Kingston, has become a national **shrine**.

African Independence

During Garvey's lifetime, his plans for an independent African state seemed far-fetched. Many governments thought that Garvey was a troublemaker, and he was accused of giving black people false hopes. But his ideas inspired many Africans to fight for equality, and today most African countries have become independent.

In 1920, UNIA members elected Marcus Garvey provisional president of Africa. More than 50 000 people took part in a parade through the streets of Harlem to celebrate the event.

JACQUES COUSTEAU

Born 1910

Although he is best known as an undersea explorer, Jacques Cousteau has spent much of his life campaigning on behalf of the environment and the world's wildlife.

Jacques-Yves Cousteau was born in France in 1910. When he was 20, he entered the French Naval Academy. Three years later, Cousteau joined the French navy as a second lieutenant, and was stationed at Toulon on the Mediterranean coast.

The aqualung

Over the next few years, Cousteau became interested in underwater diving. With another Frenchman, Emile Gagnan, he designed the first aqualung. This invention consisted of air cylinders containing compressed air, and a mouthpiece that fed air to a diver. Divers could descend to depths of 60 metres without having to wear heavy protective suits, and they were able to spend long periods underwater.

War hero

When the Second World War (1939-1945) began, Cousteau served with the **French Resistance**. He was a courageous fighter, and at the end of the war he was awarded the Croix de Guerre. This is one of the highest honours France can give its people.

Jacques Cousteau celebrating his 75th birthday on board his ship *Calypso*.

Pollution

Over the years people have polluted the earth, either accidentally or on purpose. Tropical rainforests have been cut down, oil tankers have spilt oil and **toxic waste** has been dumped into rivers and seas, killing fish and other wildlife. These are just some of the environmental disasters that are happening today.

Environmental groups such as Friends of the Earth and Greenpeace campaign to make the public more aware of this destruction. They hope that by gaining public support they can make our planet cleaner and safer for everyone.

Underwater films

In 1946, Cousteau founded the Undersea Research Group, which was attached to the navy. He worked on the dangerous job of clearing unexploded mines from the sea.

He also began to make scientific films underwater. Cousteau proved to be a skilled underwater photographer and, in 1957, his film *The Golden Fish* won an Academy Award for the best short film.

Exploring the oceans

During the 1950s, Cousteau went on many explorations on behalf of the National Geographic Society in his specially built **oceanographic** research ship, *Calypso.* These included an expedition to the Red Sea in 1951, and a four year survey of the world's oceans which began in 1952.

A deep sea diver using an aqualung.

Nuclear power

Nuclear power stations like the one in Japan shown here provide us with electricity, but also produce waste which is extremely **radioactive**. The waste matter is held in heavy lead or concrete **shields** to stop it poisoning people or the environment.

Environmental campaigners have often warned that the risk of a nuclear accident is too great to carry on producing energy this way. On 24 April 1986 they were nearly proved right when a **reactor** at the Chernobyl nuclear power plant in the Ukraine exploded.

The world beneath the oceans

Cousteau continued to make films, and his television programme, *The Undersea World of Jacques Cousteau*, ran for ten years all over the world. Through this programme, Cousteau was able to show people the wonderful creatures that live in the ocean.

Nuclear waste

In 1960, Cousteau became involved in a campaign to stop the planned dumping of nuclear waste in the Mediterranean Sea. Governments listened to him because they knew he cared about the environment, and the plans to dump the waste were dropped.

Cousteau also protested against nuclear energy and nuclear weapons. He believed that nuclear energy was dangerous, and worried there would be an environmental tragedy if countries continued to dump their nuclear waste in the oceans.

Jacques Cousteau preparing to descend 100 metres underwater to study marine life.

Protecting the environment

Cousteau knew that his international fame as an underwater explorer and film maker could help environmental groups. Over the next 35 years he supported many causes that campaigned to protect the environment and animal and marine life. In particular, he has campaigned for the **conservation** of the sea-bed, and to protect the environment of Antarctica.

Tests in the Pacific

In 1995, Cousteau protested to the French government about their plans to test nuclear bombs in the Pacific Ocean. The tests went ahead, but the French authorities have decided, due to pressure from governments all over the world, that there will be no more tests.

Fighting on

At an age when most people are content to retire, Jacques Cousteau is still fighting and campaigning on behalf of environmental causes. His long life as an explorer, inventor, film maker and campaigner has shown the world how fascinating and wonderful life is in the depths of the ocean, but also how we need to work to protect it.

Jacques Cousteau addressing crowds at a rally to campaign against nuclear tests in the Pacific.

NELSON MANDELA

Born 1918

For over 50 years, Nelson Mandela campaigned for the **abolition** of apartheid in South Africa. He spent 27 years in prison. Four years after his release in 1990, he was elected president of South Africa.

White people began to move to South Africa in the seventeenth century. The first settlers were Dutch, and they were followed by people from France and Britain. The native South Africans lived off the land, but the Europeans took the land from them and claimed it as their own.

In time, the Europeans formed a government that took control of a country where most people were black. Many white people, especially those of Dutch descent who were called Afrikaners, believed that black people were inferior.

System of apartheid

The Afrikaners insisted on **racial** separation. They believed that black and white people should live separate lives. In 1948, they established the policy of apartheid, which means separate development. Apartheid denied black people the right to any say in how their country was governed, or where they lived.

Nelson Mandela's fight to end apartheid was one of the greatest political campaigns this century.

The townships

White people lived in cities, while black people lived in **townships**, or in the homelands, which were country areas set aside for black South Africans by the government. They were overcrowded, and the Africans who lived there lost their South African **citizenship**.

Black law firm

Nelson Mandela was born in Natal in 1918. He was the son of the chief of the Tembu tribe. Nelson was sent away to school when he was nine years old. He worked hard, and won a place at university to study law. He qualified in 1942, and went to live in Johannesburg, where he set up the first black law firm in South Africa. Mandela tried to help black people by representing them in court and fighting for their rights.

The ANC

The African National Congress (ANC) was established in 1912. Its aim was to bring together all Africans in their fight for equal rights. In 1925, the ANC adopted a flag of black (for the people), green (for the land), and gold (for the resources). For the next 35 years the ANC campaigned for **democracy** in South Africa, but in 1960 it was banned by the government as an unlawful organization.

Apartheid in action. Separate toilets for black and white people in Johannesburg.

Joining the ANC

In 1944, Mandela joined the African National **Congress**, and became one of its leaders. He organized protests against the government and led peaceful demonstrations against **segregation**. The government responded by attacking protesters and arresting thousands of ANC supporters, but the demonstrations continued throughout the 1950s.

Spear of the Nation

In 1960 thousands of Africans gathered for an anti-apartheid demonstration in Sharpeville. The Africans were unarmed, but the police opened fire on them, and 69 people were shot dead. The government banned the ANC, and Mandela realized that the days of peaceful protest were over.

After much discussion the ANC decided to form a **guerrilla** army called Umkhonto we Sizwe (Spear of the Nation). This organization wanted to overthrow the white government. They began planning acts of **sabotage,** and carried out attacks on power plants and military and government buildings, especially those connected with the policy of apartheid.

Life imprisonment

Mandela was actively involved in Umkhonto we Sizwe, and in 1962 he was arrested and sentenced to five years' imprisonment. But the government wanted to keep him in prison for life. Their chance came in 1963 when police raided a house in the suburb of Rivonia in Johannesburg, and found guns and equipment belonging to Umkhonto we Sizwe.

The courtyard at Robben Island.
Nelson Mandela is one of the prisoners sewing prison clothes in the line on the right.

Boycott

Nelson Mandela's dedication to the campaign to end apartheid inspired people all over the world to support the cause. The South African economy suffered as countries **boycotted** South African goods. South Africa was expelled from the 1964 Olympic Games, and artists and entertainers refused to visit the country.

President of South Africa

In 1993, Mandela and De Klerk won the Nobel Peace Prize for their efforts to end apartheid peacefully. Mandela went on to lead the ANC in talks with the white government, which resulted in the first democratic elections ever held in South Africa. The ANC won easily and, in 1994, Nelson Mandela became the first president of the new, multi-racial South Africa.

Anti-apartheid movement

The imprisoned Mandela was charged with plotting to overthrow the government, and sentenced to life imprisonment. He spent the next 27 years in prison, many of them under harsh conditions at Robben Island, a barren wasteland off the coast of Cape Town. But even here Mandela spoke out against the injustice of apartheid. He had huge support from the people of South Africa, and from people all over the world.

Freedom at last

From 1980, international pressure to end racial **discrimination** increased. Finally, in 1990, the government lifted its ban on the ANC. On 11 February that year, the government leader, President F W de Klerk, released Nelson Mandela from prison.

All over the world, millions of people switched on their television sets and saw the 71-year-old Nelson Mandela walk out of prison.

President Mandela addresses an international conference in Johannesburg in 1993.

MARTIN LUTHER KING

1929–1968

Martin Luther King is one of the greatest **civil rights** campaigners in history. He dedicated his life to the fight for equal rights for black Americans.

Slavery was **abolished** in the United States of America at the end of the American Civil War in 1865. But for most black people the struggle for freedom was just beginning. Over the next hundred years laws were passed in the southern states of America depriving black people of their civil rights. They were not allowed to vote, own property or use the same toilets, parks, cinemas, libraries or restaurants as white people.

Baptist minister

Martin Luther King was born in 1929 in Georgia, one of the southern states of America. When he was 15, King went to college in Atlanta on a programme for gifted students. He wanted to be a **Baptist** minister like his father and grandfather. He gained his degree in **divinity** in 1948, and then went to the University of Boston where he studied for a **doctorate**. It was there that he read about the Indian leader, Mahatma Gandhi, who changed conditions for Indian people without using violence.

Civil rights activist Martin Luther King. Under his leadership, the civil rights movement ended **segregation** in the southern states of America.

Rosa Parks sitting in the front of a city bus in Alabama in 1955.

Bus boycott

King had been in Alabama for about a year when black people organized a protest against segregation on public buses. A black woman called Rosa Parks sat in a seat saved for white people, and refused to move. She was arrested, because in Alabama black people were forced to sit at the back of the buses. People were outraged and **boycotted** the bus company. King became involved in the boycott, and was chosen by the protesters as their leader.

Southern racism

While he was in Boston, King met a music student called Coretta Scott. They married in 1953, and went to live in the southern United States. They both knew how difficult life was for black people in the south, but for them it was home. King accepted a position of **pastor** at a Baptist church in Montgomery, Alabama – one of the most **racist** states in the USA.

Victorious outcome

Black people in Alabama were prepared to walk long distances rather than travel on the buses. They demanded that the bus company let them sit where they wanted. The bus company held out for a year, but it lost so much money that it was forced to give in to the protesters. The campaigners were triumphant and the civil rights movement gained a famous victory.

Civil rights

When Martin Luther King talked about civil rights, he meant the right to own property, the right to speak freely, the right not to be imprisoned without being charged with an offence, and the right to be treated fairly.

In May 1953 police in Alabama set their dogs on civil rights protesters.

Nobel Prize Winner

The Nobel Prize was named after Alfred Bernhard Nobel, a Swedish chemist who invented dynamite. When he died, Nobel stated in his will that his fortune should go towards setting up a system of awards that would be given every year to people who made great contributions in the fields of physics, chemistry, medicine, literature and world peace. The Nobel Peace Prize was first awarded in 1901. Since then some of the most famous people this century have won the award. Martin Luther King won it in 1964. In 1993 Nelson Mandela and F W de Klerk jointly won it for peacefully ending white rule in South Africa.

Non-violent protest

In 1957 King helped start the Southern Christian Leaders Conference (SCLC) which brought together all the civil rights groups. He travelled all over the country giving lectures to tell his followers that the best way for black people to win equal rights was to protest in a non-violent way.

For whites only

In 1960 King agreed to support sit-ins by blacks in whites-only restaurants in Georgia and Alabama. When black protesters entered the restaurants, they were attacked by angry white people. The events were shown on television, and people all over America saw how the non-violent black protesters were treated. King was arrested and sentenced to four months' hard labour. But there was a massive public outcry and, with the help of the President of the United States, John F Kennedy, King was released.

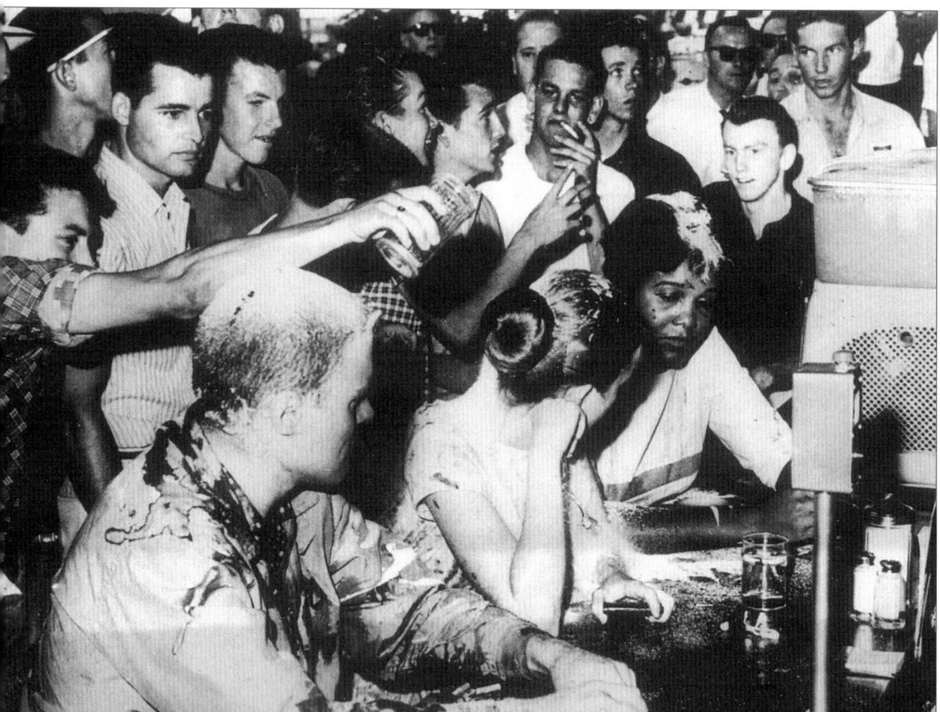

People pouring sugar, ketchup and mustard over a black girl and her white friends in a whites-only restaurant in Jackson, Mississippi.

I have a dream…

In August 1963 King organized a march to Washington, the home of the United States government, to demand equal justice for all people. Over 250 000 people marched with him and heard him give his famous 'I have a dream' speech. In this speech, King spoke of a society where racism and **discrimination** did not exist.

I have a dream that one day on the red hills of Georgia the sons of former slaves and the sons of former slave-owners will be able to sit down together at the table of brotherhood. I have a dream that my four little children will one day live in a nation where they will not be judged by the colour of their skin but by the content of their character.

Martin Luther King speaks to the crowd at the Washington rally in 1963.

Civil Rights Bill

The following year the United States **Congress** passed the Civil Rights Bill, which made segregation and discrimination in public places illegal. In the same year, Martin Luther King was awarded the Nobel Peace Prize for fighting injustice without violence.

The promised land

King continued to campaign, turning his attention to solving problems such as poverty and unemployment. In April 1968, he went to Memphis. In his speech on 4 April he told his followers, 'I may not get to the promised land with you, but I want you to know tonight that we as a people will.' The next day he was shot dead. Martin Luther King fought all his life for equal rights for black Americans, and achieved so much without once using violence.

Glossary

Abolish To put an end to something, for example slavery.

Armoury A place where weapons and armour are kept.

Assassinate To murder a person by a surprise attack.

Baptist A member of the Protestant Christian Church who believes in baptism.

Boycott To refuse to have anything to do with a person or organisation.

Caulking Making the bottom of a boat or ship watertight by filling in the cracks between the planks.

Citizenship The right to be a member of a country and to live there.

Civil disobedience Breaking the law without using violence.

Civil rights The rights of everyone to live and speak freely, to own property and to be treated fairly.

Colonies Land settled and governed by people from another part of the world.

Congress A group of people who make the laws of a country.

Conservation The protection of the environment.

Cruise missile A small low-flying weapon with a nuclear warhead.

Democracy A country ruled by a government chosen by the people who live there.

Deport To force someone to leave a country.

Discrimination Unfair treatment of a person because of their race, colour, religion or sex.

Divinity The study of God.

Doctorate The highest level of degree.

Emigrate To move to a new country.

Excise Taxes on goods such as alcohol.

Extremist A person with strong political ideas who is prepared to use violence.

French Resistance A secret organisation which fought against the Nazi occupation of France in the Second World War.

Fraud Cheating or lying to gain money.

Guerrilla A fighter who wages war by ambush and surprise attack.

Illiteracy Being unable to read and write.

Insurrection A rebellion against a government.

Martyr Someone who suffers or dies for their beliefs.

Militant A person who uses violence to further a cause.

Munitions Military stores and equipment.

Nationalist Someone who wants their country to be free of foreign rule.

Non-co-operation Refusing to work with other people or countries as a protest against them.

Oceanography The study of the ocean.

Partition To divide a country into separate areas.

Pastor A clergyman or priest.

Penal colonies Prisons in foreign countries where convicts were sent.

Prow The front of a ship or boat.

Racial Dividing people into races according to how they look.

Racial harassment Treating people badly because of their race.

Racist Believing that people of some races are better than others.

Radical An extreme political view.

Radioactive Something that gives off harmful nuclear rays.

Reactor A container in which chemical reactions produce nuclear energy.

Regiment A large number of soldiers in an army.

Republic A state governed by the people or their elected representatives, not by a king or queen.

Sabotage To destroy or disrupt.

Segregation Forcing people of different races to live apart.

Shield A strong barrier around a nuclear reactor to stop dangerous radioactive rays escaping.

Shrine A place that is important to a religion or connected with a famous person or event.

Suffragette A woman who campaigned for suffrage (the right to vote) to be given to women.

Tannery A place where animal hides and skins are made into leather.

Townships South African towns where black and coloured Africans were forced to live before the end of apartheid.

Toxic waste Poisonous chemicals that can damage or kill plants and animals.

Treason The crime of betraying your country, usually by trying to overthrow the government.

INDEX